To

Mary A. Pennington

Dreams of Yesterday and Hopes for Tomorrow

A Book of Poetry
by Mary A. Pennington

VANTAGE PRESS
New York / Los Angeles / Chicago

FIRST EDITION

Published by Vantage Press, Inc.
516 West 34th Street, New York, New York 10001

Manufactured in the United States of America
ISBN: 0-533-08529-2

Library of Congress Catalog Card No.: 88-90144

Dedication

To Mom and Dad, who are the reason for all my dreams of yesterday. And because they raised me up in the right way, I now have sweet hopes for tomorrow. Although Dad has gone on to his reward, his memory still gives me many inspirations.

To my husband and seven children, without whose love and encouragement, I could not have continued my writing.

To St. Mary Hospital, where I worked so long; to all my supervisors and co-workers, who stood by me faithfully while I was sick. To Annapolis Hospital, where I have been a patient so many times, and to all the staff there. Also, to my doctor, Roy W. Matthews, Jr., who has not only been my doctor, but also a good friend. To all my brothers and sisters, but especially to my brother, Billy, who has been so faithful in giving me a call almost every night.

But most of all to God, who saw fit to reach down and save a sinner like me.

To each and everyone, I owe my deepest gratitude, but to God I owe everything. For without him, there would be no *Dreams of Yesterday and Hopes for Tomorrow*. I love him above everything.

Contents

Preface

I gave my heart and soul to God in 1984 and joined the Old Regular Baptist Church of Ypsilanti in 1985. Since then he has been my strength through all my sickness. He's the only friend I have to go to. Even in the darkest hours of the night he's always there for me to lean on.

I hope some of these poems will be a blessing to someone and make them stop and think that our life on earth is but a short span and without God there is nothing. He's our all and all. If just one poem can make one person wonder where he will spend eternity, then my work will not have been in vain. May God bless each and every one of us is my prayer. I love you all.

Memories of Yesterday

Today I went back to the country,
  to the green and rolling hills.
All the times I used to play there,
  I remember those good times still.
There's the place our house was sitting,
  but it's not there anymore,
But in my memory I can see it,
  with Mom and Daddy at the door.

I recall the white picket fence,
  with roses blooming all around,
And that little old grape arbor,
  now it, too, was torn down.
A big new house was standing
  where our little house had been.
My heart was weeping as I stood there,
  remembering childhood years again.

Our little house was filled with love,
  for God was dwelling there within
We were taught to have respect,
  just the way it should have been.
My eyes began to fill with tears,
  as I remembered so many things,
An old rocking chair on the porch,
  where Mama used to sit and sing.

My heart was filled with sadness,
  oh, I missed those times so much
Mom and Daddy's gentle voice,
  their sweet and tender touch.
Lord, the good times are all gone,
  nothing is the same any more.
They've both gone to live with Jesus
  over on sweet Heaven's shore.

All the Wasted Years

Today I went back home again,
  and this is what I found.
The little place where I was raised,
  the house had fallen to the ground.
That old tree I used to play in,
  its branches were all bowed.
All the precious years I've wasted
  sure don't make me very proud.

The precious years I've wasted,
  oh how I'm crying for them now.
I should have found a way
  to go back home again somehow.
The mom and dad I left behind,
  I'd love to see them once again.
But they've both gone to Heaven
  where I'll cause them no more pain.

They waited for me for so long;
  each day to God they prayed
That their son would come home
  and quit his wandering ways.
I wonder if they're waiting
  in their mansion over there.
Know that I've cried a million times
  for wasting all those precious years.

Days of My Youth

The good times of my youth,
  I remember them so well.
A kind, loving dad and
  the stories he would tell.
We never had much money,
  but we were rich as could be.
The days of my youth are
  now sweet memories to me.

Though we had many chores,
  there was still time for play.
We'd work that much harder
  to get them out of the way,
Then we'd head for the hills,
  from the trees we would swing.
In the days of my youth, life
  made our little hearts sing.

We didn't have all the things
  our children have today,
But we were still happy with
  little games we could play,
Like ring around the roses,
  and hide and go seek.
Those days of my youth left
  old sweet memories so deep.

The sweetest times of all
  were around Daddy's knees.
By the fireside at night,
  all our troubles would cease.
Oh, I'd give everything to
  bring those times back today.
But the days of my youth,
  have all vanished away.

A Stroll down Memory Lane

My mind just wandered back today
  for a little stroll down memory lane.
I thought of how things used to be,
  knew they'd never be that way again.

Everyone knew each other for miles around,
  always said hello each time they'd meet,
But now although it seems a shame,
  you don't know your neighbor down the street.

An old farmer plowing in the fields
  always took the time to stop and chat.
But now everyone just walks on by,
  they're too busy doing this and that.

A group of kids would get together
  and take a walk beneath the stars.
But now they just want to be alone,
  out riding around in their old cars.

Oh, but who can we blame for that,
  how can we expect them to be so good?
Parents are too busy with their own lives,
  to raise their children like they should.

They won't take their kids to church today,
  they say they can't make them behave.
If they'd use the rod, not spoil the child,
  there'd be more love in this world today.

Hills of Old Kentucky

Today I went back once again,
  to my early childhood home
In my mind I still recall,
  the places where I loved to roam
The dark and rolling hills,
  the valleys deep and green
Oh, the hills of old Kentucky,
Are the prettiest places I've ever seen.

Among the little pawpaw trees,
  we made our playhouse on the hill
Separating the rooms with rocks,
  some of them are standing still
We made our little kids from sticks,
  dressed them up so clean and neat
There around our little table,
  we'd say grace before we'd eat.

All the little paths we'd walk
  I remember them yet so well
As we'd go to hunt the cows,
  listening for that old cow bell
It seemed I heard Daddy's voice,
  as it echoed through the hills
Gently calling for us to come,
  oh but now everything was still.

For no more we'll hear his voice,
  on a hill he's laid to rest
Among his friends and loved ones,
  in the place he loved the best
Those precious childhood memories,
  now so much to me they mean
The hills of old Kentucky,
Are still the prettiest places I've seen.

Little Churches in Kentucky

Oh, I'd love to go back once again
to the hills of old Kentucky
Where as a little child
there I spent my younger days.
With Mom and Dad we lived
on a farm in the mountains.
Yes I wish we could go back
to the good old-fashioned ways.

There was nothing for me then
like the hills of old Kentucky
To keep a child so happy,
make him feel so alive and so free.
At a little country church
that sat way down in the valley,
It was there I learned the meaning
of what God's love meant to me.

There're so many things out there
to tempt our children today.
Have them raised the way I was,
there's nothing I wouldn't give
If they'd only learn the meaning
of what real love's all about.
A dear old mom and dad like mine,
to really teach them how to live.

They'd get us all dressed up,
take us to church on Sunday,
Where they sang and shouted his praises
in the good old-fashioned way.
If we had more churches now
like they had in old Kentucky
There'd be more kids in church
than on the streets today.

My Home in the Country

There's a place back in the hills
  where I'd love to go again
And smell the honeysuckle
  that blooms down in the lane,
Watch the little fireflies
  as they light the starry night,
Hear the crickets chirping loudly
  underneath the pale moonlight.

Where you wake up every morning
  to a bright and sunny day,
To a good old country breakfast
  that will help you on your way.
Walking barefoot through the clover
  in the early morning dew
As you stroll down by the river
  where the water's clear and blue.

The smell of wild red roses
  that grow so pretty on the hills
Makes you feel like you're in Heaven
  with the singing whippoorwills
Where you sit out on the front porch
  when the evening sun goes down
To hear that good old country music,
  friends would come from miles around.

I miss that little country home
  so much since I moved away.
And I'll keep on going back
  till they take me back to stay.
Back to that little country church
  my parents took me for so long.
Where they'll lay me down to rest;
  then I'll know I'm safe at home.

Sweet Memories So Dear

What would we do without the memories
  of things we hold so dear and sweet.
The day our baby took his first step,
  or when he cut his two front teeth.
Those first memories are the best ones,
  they're by far the hardest to forget.
No matter how old your children are,
  those precious things you remember yet.

God saw fit to give me seven little ones,
  so I've got plenty of loving memories
For each little one was different,
  even a stranger's eyes could see.
One of them could look at you so sweet
  and melt your heart with so much joy.
That little girl with all her innocence,
  or that mischievious sneaky little boy.

The day each one started school,
  as they marched so bravely out the door,
They looked so small you couldn't help
  but want to hold them close to you once more.
The little pictures they would draw,
  bring them home to you with so much pride,
Just looking at them sometimes now
  still brings teardrops to my eyes.

All the little hand prints they left
  upon your freshly painted walls,
All the times we yelled at them
  for bouncing their little rubber balls.
But if you're like me, I bet you wish
  they were all little once again.
Then your heart was filled with joy,
  now it's filled with heartaches and pain.

Precious Memories of Home

There's many happy memories
of my precious childhood years.
Mom and Dad were always there
to take away all my fears.
If only I could go back again
and have things be that way,
Be a little girl once more,
just now learning how to play.

Times were hard back then
and things were always rough.
Daddy worked so very hard,
made sure we always had enough.
But we had something then,
worth more to me than gold—
An old-fashioned Christian home,
where God's love did unfold.

They told me about a Savior
who died upon a rugged cross,
Who shed his precious blood
to save a world from being lost.
I'm so proud I was a part
of that little Christian home,
So glad I had a mom and dad
who always taught me right from wrong.

Lord, things are not the same
since Daddy's gone away.
That little home is now so lonesome,
we miss him more and more each day.
But the years that Daddy gave me,
from me they'll never part,
And precious memories of my home
I'll always hold them in my heart.

When I'm in the Valley

Sometimes I wonder, dear Jesus,
am I worthy to be one of your own?
I get so far down in the valley,
it's so hard to find my way home.

It's hard to find the words to tell you
just what it is I'm wanting to say.
But I guess you know what I'm needing
before I even kneel down to pray.

It's hard to let my light shine for you
when I feel this way in my heart.
But my faith for you keeps on lingering,
from your sweet love I never will part.

For you said you'd never forsake me
and I know your sweet promise you'll keep.
You'll always be there when I need you,
wipe the tears from my eyes when I weep.

You give me a small glimpse of Heaven
and Jacob's ladder hanging so high.
If I take one step at a time, Jesus,
I'll reach Heaven someday, by and by.

A Tribute to a Little Church

There's a little church I go to,
each time I seem to love it more
Everyone meets you with a smile
as you walk in through the door.
Although I don't belong there,
I feel I do down in my heart,
For Heaven is our only goal and
there we'll never have to part.

We have the same love for our God
way down deep inside our soul.
A home is waiting for us all
where the streets are made of gold.
They always make me feel so welcome,
they never seem to leave me out.
It's so hard to hold yourself,
when dear old mothers start to shout.

Just a handshake and a smile
is all it really takes to start
To make some poor lost sinner
feel God's love down in his heart.
That old time gospel singing
to me grows sweeter every day.
Their voices all blend together,
God just seems to lead the way.

Since I was just a little girl,
a sweeter sound I've never heard
Than an old-fashioned preacher,
preaching God's holy word.
If we all would walk together
with our Savior by our side,
In that little old church house,
with God's love we can abide.

Mother

Just a sweet and simple woman
 with her plain old-fashioned ways.
Always there to guide my footsteps
 as I spent my childhood days.

Always there to be a comfort
 when I'd rise to start the day.
Then she'd smile and gently hold me
 before she'd send me out to play.

She was always there to teach me,
 to gently wipe away my tears,
There to help me with my problems
 as I grew to teenage years.

With her caring arms around me
 and her love so true and strong,
She was always there to go to
 when everything turned out wrong.

I'll always love her very much
 and for me there is no other
That can ever take the place
 of my dear old-fashioned Mother.

A Mother's Love

A mother is someone
  who we know will always care.
No matter what we seem to do,
  her love is always there
To guide our little footsteps,
  teach us wrong from right,
There to listen to our prayers,
  as she kisses us good night.

There to wipe away our tears
  when everything goes wrong
The best friend we could find,
    whose love is always strong,
She goes without a lot of things,
  just like she's done before
So her children will be happy,
  She'll let it go once more.

And as we grow to teenage years,
  we begin to realize
The love a mother has
  shines deeper in her eyes.
Every time that we go out,
  she waits there by the door
To know her children are all in
  and safe at home once more.

As the years take hold of her,
  her dark hair turns to gray.
We know her love will still be there
  to cheer us on our way.
The bond she's always had for us
  is still there just as strong.
There's nothing like a mother's love
  to make a house a home.

A Mother's Prayer

Lord, another warning you gave me
as this old body was burning with pain.
I prayed to my God up in Heaven,
let me live to see my children again.

Let me once more tell them of Jesus,
who gave his life upon Calvary
As he hung there between earth and Heaven
to save a wretched sinner like me.

The God who loved his Son so dearly
sent him down here to die on the cross
But this old world has grown so wicked,
it's so hard when your prayers seem so lost.

Lord, let me live a while longer,
my loved ones are still out in sin.
Let me be a light shining for them,
Just one little lost sheep might come in.

Oh, children, can't you hear Mother praying,
no matter how far in sin you may be
At the foot of the cross he can save you,
for just look at what he's done for me.

Mother's Dream

Mother has always had her
  own special dream
Of the one thing she's
  wanted right from the start.
It's a little log cabin
  way back in the hills.
A home she's been wanting
  with all of her heart.

That little log cabin,
  she's always yearned for.
Way back in the hills
  beside a small stream
Where the roses are blooming
  and the whippoorwills call.
To have that little log cabin,
  that's been Mother's dream.

She wants nothing fancy,
  no diamonds or gold,
Or a big roomy mansion,
  to be all her own.
Just what she yearns for,
  what she deserves is
That little log cabin
  that would be her own home.

She may never have it
  while in this old world.
She'll just go on dreaming
  till her life here is done.
Someday God will reward her
  for her work here below.
He'll give her that cabin;
  it will be her own home.

Mother's Light

This life that I'm living
  now has a new meaning.
Every day now is filled
  with something so new.
I find there's new strength
  to do more things for Jesus,
But I want Mother's light
  to have new meaning for you.

Please let Mother's light
  shine bright upon you.
You might be surprised
  at what you can do,
For Jesus may bless you
  more and more every day
If you'll let Mother's light
  be there to show you the way.

I've prayed many times
  for God's will to be done.
What he'd have me to do
  in the name of his Son.
Please let my light shine
  so someone can see.
Let my children know
  that he's set Mother free.

When your mother is gone,
  just follow the light,
You'll not lose the way,
  she'll leave it so bright.
Always remember the love
  she had for his Son.
Holding to Mother's light,
  you'll never walk it alone.

Mother's Sleeping at Last

When my time comes to go and
  you lay me down to rest,
Take me back to the place
  you know I love the best.
As they lay the sod over me,
  children, I'll be all right.
I'll just be trying out
  the bed God gave me tonight.

Have them put my grave
  underneath an old tree
Where I know the little birds
  will be singing over me.
When you visit my grave,
  honey, I'll know it's you.
If you want to bring flowers,
  just a little rose will do.

When you kneel by my grave,
  will you sing me a song?
I'll know the sound of your voice,
  you know I've loved it so long.
You've been my companion
  for so many years.
I'll just be waiting for you,
  please don't shed any tears.

When the snow starts to come,
  don't you worry about me.
Safe and warm in the arms
  of sweet Jesus I'll be.
No more lying awake,
  children worrying about you.
It will be the first time
  I'll sleep the night through.

Always Needing Mother

No matter how many years go by,
  or how far away you seem to roam,
There'll come a time you'll realize,
  there just can't be no place like home.

With Mother baking in the kitchen,
  Daddy sitting in his favorite chair
Watching all the baseball games on TV,
  somehow Mother never seemed to care.

Sometimes we wish we could go back,
  when all us kids were small again.
When we would fall and scrape our chins
  and Mother could kiss away our pain.

I guess we never get too old,
  to need our mother once in a while
To hear her soft and gentle voice,
  see her face light up with a smile.

Hear her tell us that she loves us
  as she looks to God above.
We know there's nothing under Heaven
  that can take the place of Mother's love.

A Lonely Mother's Prayer

There's a dear old mother
who's just sitting all alone,
Patiently waiting for the day
her precious son will come home,
Longing so much to see him,
her own pride and joy,
Praying God in his Heaven
would stay with her boy.

Dear God, watch over him,
keep him under your care.
Keep holding to his hand,
while he's over there
Fighting for his country,
the sweet land of the free.
And Lord, if it be your will,
please bring him home to me.

She takes down his picture,
the one that's so dear
And crying so silently,
she holds it to her so near.
To her own broken heart,
there all alone in the night
She prays once again to God,
"Let him please be all right.

"If you'll let him come home
to be with me once again,
Then my aching heart
will be free from all pain."
She'll always go on praying,
until the war has been won.
When she can once again
hold her own darling son.

The Mother Your Children Need

Honey, you're my daughter.
  I love you with all my heart.
Won't you make your peace with God
  so we'll never have to part?
Those little ones he gave to you,
  he put their care within your hands.
But can you teach them right from wrong
  if you yourself don't understand?

When they ask a question about God,
  do you just shrug and turn away?
Just put your arms around them and
  this is all you have to say,
"Baby, someone loves you,
  more than Mommy does, I know.
He just gave you to me for a while,
  so I could help you as you grow."

So get God's love within your heart;
  what a difference there will be.
There'll be a change in Mommy
  in such a way that they can see.
You will find it's not so hard,
  when you're not doing it all alone
For he'll be there to help you,
  'cause he loves those little ones.

Before you go to sleep each night,
  always say this little prayer.
"God, watch over them and keep them,
  for I place them in your care.
Please let me live to raise them
  in the way you'd have them be.
Make me the kind of mother
  that my mother was to me."

A Change in Mother

While standing on the banks of the river,
  I saw a sight I'd never seen before.
My old sainted mother went under,
  she came back up praising the Lord.

On her face there was a smile so pretty,
  as the tears so freely did flow
I remember her words so clearly,
  "Thank you, Lord, for saving my soul."

As a child I couldn't understand it,
  in that old water, why she had to go in.
That's the first time that God whispered to me;
  he said, "I've washed away your mother's sins."

I said, "Lord, she's already the best one
  anyone could ever find on this earth."
But there was a new change in Mother
  since God had given her a new birth.

Now today as I go under for Jesus,
  all these things come back to my mind.
First of all I'll thank God for Salvation,
  then for giving me a mother like mine.

Daddy Marked the Way

Oh, I'm going to a beautiful country
  over on that beautiful shore
I'll walk through the portals of Glory,
  where I'll see troubles and trials no more.

There'll be no detours on my journey,
  for the way is narrow and straight.
With faith the path will be easy;
  Love's the key that will open the gate.

The road map is the Bible Daddy left me,
  he marked each page with his tears
It may be old, but to me it is priceless,
  It's been a guide for me all these years.

Oh, Daddy, I've now met your Savior,
  the one you loved for so long.
All the prayers you prayed for me, Daddy,
  they reached Heaven, now I'm coming home

I'll meet you someday over yonder
  and shake hands with you once more.
You'll be smiling as you come to meet me,
  we'll be together on Heaven's bright shore.

Daddy's Footsteps

We were sitting there with Daddy
  one night before he died
And as I looked at him
  I knew he'd soon be satisfied.
He'd been so good to us,
  taught us right through all the years
And as these words came to me,
  I wrote them through my tears.

Lord, let me walk the path
  my daddy walked each day.
He gave his life to Jesus, walked
  the straight and narrow way.
His faith never faltered,
  God kept him in his care.
If I follow Daddy's footsteps,
  someday I'll meet him there.

Yes, I'll follow Daddy's footsteps
  each step of the way,
For he promised I'd reach Heaven,
  some sweet and happy day.
There we'll walk hand in hand
  with our loved ones up above.
I'll follow Daddy's footsteps,
  for he paved the way with love.

That old Bible marks the
  way to that eternal home
Where Heaven will be waiting
  just a little farther on.
I'll never lose the way;
  he'll be waiting there for me.
As long as Daddy's footsteps
  are there for me to see.

Does Daddy Still Pray?

I can't help but wonder,
with all the snow on the ground
As it covers the grave,
where Daddy's sleeping so sound
Is it just a blanket
God put there to keep him warm
While he's sleeping so peaceful,
safely now from all storms?

Does Daddy still miss us;
does he still for us pray?
Is he still watching for us
there in Heaven today?
Where I know that he's happy,
at home now with God
For he's walking on streets
where sweet Angels have trod.

Is he talking to you, Jesus
about the ones he left behind?
All the prayers I still remember,
from that old daddy of mine,
The songs that he taught us
through the years they still ring,
But he's joined a new band,
around the throne he now sings.

Does he still talk so softly,
have that same gentle touch
That we all loved so dearly
and still miss very much?
But until we get to Heaven,
where we'll see him once more
Tell him to keep on praying, we'll
meet him on that bright shore.

Daddy's First Christmas in Heaven

It's almost Christmas time again
  and everyone is full of cheer.
Gifts underneath the tree
  for friends we love so dear.
But this year a face is missing
  around the fire at night.
Daddy's now singing Christmas carols
  in Heaven's soft candlelight.

His Christmas here on earth
  was always filled with so much joy
As he tried to figure out
  just the right thing for each boy.
There was never any doubt,
  for the little girls he knew what to buy
And I know he's thinking of us
  there at his Christmas in the sky.

That brand-new harp he gets,
  I bet he'll play it loud and clear.
As he sings with all the angels,
  we can feel his love so dear
And with his brand new halo
  he earned while here on earth,
He will have a real good Christmas,
  God will give him what he's worth.

While he's at his Christmas party,
  his mind will be on me and you.
That we won't miss him very much,
  our Christmas here won't be so blue.
And, Dad, we know the gift you want
  is so special to you this year
Is to tell you that someday,
  we'll all meet you over there.

Christmas without Daddy

Christmastime was always special
  it meant so very much to me
To see all the family gathered
  around our little Christmas tree.
But this year it is so lonely,
  for we miss someone so dear.
For Daddy won't be with us
  at Christmastime this year.

Will Daddy have a Christmas
  like he did when he was here?
Will he have lots of laughter,
  will the angels bring him cheer?
Will he miss us all down here?
  Lord you know we loved him so.
Oh, Christmas without Daddy,
  will be lonesome we all know.

Mama tries so hard to keep
  us all filled with Christmas cheer.
The way Daddy would have wanted,
  if he were still with us down here.
But the angels are so lucky,
  they have him to sing for them.
And our Christmas without Daddy,
  for us will be a lonely time.

Home with Mom and Dad

Back in the hills of old Kentucky,
where I grew up on a little farm
Mom and Dad both worked so hard
to make me feel so safe and warm.

I loved to help them in the garden,
while we raised the things we ate
And helping Mother in the kitchen
always made me feel so great.

Dad would come in from the fields
after he'd been working all day long.
I'd help him as he'd finish the chores and
hope God would keep him healthy and strong.

But I soon grew up and moved away
from that little farm I loved so much.
Oh, no one knows how much I miss it
or long for Mom and Dad's gentle touch.

But someday I'll go back and stay
when they lay me down to rest.
With Mom and Dad I'll be at home
on that little farm I love the best.

A Gift from Mom and Dad

As I lie here thinking of
  all the mistakes I've made,
I've only myself to blame 'cause
  a good foundation was laid.
Mom and Dad were always there
  to teach me what was right.
Lord, forgive me if I'm
  too blind to see the light.

Don't let them feel the blame
  if I should go astray
So many things keep tempting me
  as I travel on my way.
Satan's standing on every corner,
  just holding out his hand.
Give me strength to turn away
  and for my Jesus stand.

Give me faith to walk the way
  my parents paved for me
They put me ever in your care
  and prayed that I would be
Ready to meet their Savior
  when life on earth shall cease
And have a home in Heaven
  that's been waiting there for me.

When I reach my home
  over on that other shore,
Mom and Dad will be waiting
  to meet me at the door.
I'll put my arms around them,
  be sure to let them know
How I thank them for my Christian home
  they gave me here below.

A Tribute to Mom and Dad

For fifty years you've been together,
  through the good times and the bad.
You've toiled and raised your children
  with all the love and faith you had.

All through the years we still remember
  what that faith and love can do.
It's always made us stop and wonder
  what we would have done without you.

Sometimes our hearts get heavy
  and burdens seem to much to bear.
That's when we need to talk to someone,
  it seems you both are always there.

At times we know we disappoint you
  by all the things we say and do.
But just remember, Mom and Dad,
  your love and faith will see us through.

So if there's not another thing,
  your children can say or do,
We want to say, "We thank the Lord
  for giving us a mom and dad like you."

A Tribute to My Daughter

Today you're getting married
as a symbol of your love.
May the Lord look down and bless you
from his Mansion up above.
It won't always be a bed of roses,
but if you both will do your best,
Always think about each other,
then your love can stand the test.

When you walk down the aisle,
walk it with one thing in mind.
This was the way that God intended,
for man and woman all the time.
Some may say that it's old fashioned,
but in your heart it's what you feel.
You've been together for some time,
you know this love is for real.

When little problems come along,
don't give up like people do.
Just put your trust in Jesus,
he'll help you see them through.
Talk things over with each other,
everything you both must share.
That's what marriage is all about,
showing each other that you care.

My Wandering Children

When I go to bed each night
I always say this little prayer.
God, will you watch over me,
keep me ever in your care.
Then before I close my eyes,
and gently drift off to sleep
I think of all my children,
so softly do I weep.

They're wandering far from you,
each going his own way.
Never thinking of tomorrow,
they're just living for today.
Let them know life down here
is just a short span on earth.
When they face eternity,
what will their soul be worth?

The pleasures they are seeking
will not last them very long—
Like a flower in the springtime
blooms a while and then it is gone
Reach out your loving arms,
bring them in from the cold.
Let them as your little sheep,
find their way into the fold.

For your sweet love can save them,
bring them safely home once more,
Set their feet upon that rock
that leads to Heaven's shore.
If they hear you, let them answer;
don't let their souls be lost.
For you gave your life for them
when you died upon the cross.

Guide My Children Home

Lord, my children are straying
so far away from the fold.
They're out there in darkness
where they're hungry and cold.
Reach out your loving arms,
protect them from every care.
Let them look up toward Heaven,
there'll be no sorrow up there.

Work your love in their heart,
let them start seeking you.
Show them what's waiting for them
after this life here is through.
Let them stand on the rock
that their forefathers stood on.
On their lips put a prayer,
in their hearts put a song.

Let them see life is worthless
if they don't have your love.
Their soul will be lost forever
if they miss sweet Heaven above.
All their treasures will vanish
just like dust in the wind,
But a better home's awaiting,
if they'll only let you come in.

Always be there to guide them
on their journey through life.
Carry all of their burdens;
set them free from all strife.
When the way gets so rugged,
they don't think they can go on,
Just take their hand in yours,
be there to help make them strong.

When they come to the river of Jordan,
let them see your arms open wide.
Let them know you will help them
safely reach the other side.
When they reach Heaven's portals,
what a reunion there'll be
With all the friends and loved ones
they've been waiting so long to see.

A Small Boy's Prayer

He was sitting alone
  on the side of his bed.
With tears in his eyes,
  he bowed his small head.
He was praying to Jesus
  to let his daddy come home,
For he missed him so much,
  he'd been gone so long.

He said, "Dear Jesus,
  Daddy answered the call
To fight for his country
  so it would not fall
And I'm trying so hard,
  to be Mommy's little man,
But I need my daddy,
  I know you'll understand.

"And if you remember,
  when you were a lad
A daddy is the best friend
  a boy ever had.
My mommy can't play catch
  and she doesn't like to fish.
Oh, I want my daddy,
  that's my biggest wish.

"So if you see my daddy
  in that big country out there,
Tell him I need him
  and how much that I care.
Just one more thing, Jesus,
  answer quick as you can.
Let my daddy come home
  to be with us again."

My Little Devil but God's Little Angel

You're just a little devil
running carefree and wild,
But you can melt this old heart
with just your tender smile.
You have so much energy
I wish some you could give
To the grandma who loves you—
it could help me to live.

God up there in his Heaven loves you
this I know.
If our hearts were like yours
he would love us all so.
You're not old enough yet
to know what sin's all about
And honey, until you are,
you're God's angel, no doubt.

So, please, Mommy and Daddy,
it's all in your hands.
For God gave him to you
to help make him a man.
So take him and mold him
the way God wants you to.
Someday he might make a way
to show Heaven to you.

Still My Little Girl

You looked so tiny and helpless,
  lying there in that old bed.
Like a baby once again
  with a cap around your head.
You were going on a journey,
  where you'd never been before
As I softly kissed you,
  told you "I loved you" once more.

I was praying to Jesus
  to keep you in his care.
You were my little girl again
  as I looked at you there.
A mother feels the pain
  more than any words can say.
But she tried so hard to be brave,
  before they wheeled you away.

Part of Mother went with you
  to the operating room.
While a part stayed behind,
  filled with sorrow and gloom,
Praying God would be there
  to guide the doctor's hand.
Let my little girl come back,
  let her be all right once again.

I know you can't understand
  just the way Mother feels.
You may be all grown up now,
  but you're just my little girl still.
When the doctor came back
  and told me everything was fine,
I thanked God for his mercy
  with all this old heart of mine.

Our Granddaughter

You're just a little flower
  in our beautiful bouquet.
With cheeks pink and rosy
  as you go about your play,
You look like an angel
  as you play your little part.
You have a special place
  down deep inside our heart.

You're a pretty little girl
  with beautiful eyes of blue.
Your smile makes our world
  seem a little brighter, too.
You're as pretty as a rose
  that blossoms in the spring,
Just a tiny rosebud
  we wouldn't trade for anything.

Tell Mommy and Daddy we're proud
  you're the little girl they chose.
In our beautiful bouquet
  you're the sweetest rose.
We thank God every day
  for our little girl so sweet.
When he made granddaughters,
  he gave us one that can't be beat.

Things That Sisters Share

Though my brother picked you out
  to help share his lonely world
He couldn't have chosen a better
  one to be his special girl.
All these years you've stayed with
  him, they've not all been good.
But you've been a loving wife,
  just like I knew you would.

To me you've been a sister;
  a lot of things we've shared
You have always been there
  just to let me know you cared.
We've shared a lot of problems,
  Lord knows there's been a few.
We've had a lot of heartaches,
  but we've had some laughter, too.

Then we had our children
  all through the coming years.
They've brought a lot of joy
  and they've caused a lot of tears.
But we've been there for each
  other, it seems, along the way.
Thank you, Sis, for being there;
  there's nothing else I can say.

Parents Are to Blame

Boys and girls don't seem to know
what's right or wrong today,
Or if they do, they don't care;
they go their merry way.
They don't care who sits at home
and worries over them.
If they don't know what morals are,
just which one of us is to blame?

We have to show them right from wrong,
or what can we expect?
They have to have a mom and dad
whom they can respect.
A home of fun and parties,
oh, how can we be proud.
They've never seen us on our knees
or even heard us pray out loud.

They should have heard of God
when they learned how to talk.
Followed in his footsteps when
they first learned how to walk.
We should have read the Bible
we kept hidden on the shelf.
When our children start to stray
we have no one to blame but ourselves.

Because of Love

Our Lord, who hung there on Calvary
  wore a crown of thorns round his head.
A spear had been driven through him,
  oh, how bright was the blood that he shed.

He looked toward his Father in Heaven,
  the blood mixed with tears in his eyes
With nothing but love in his bosom.
  "Father, forgive them," he cried.

For six long hours he hung there,
  nailed to that old rugged cross.
Oh, can't you just see how he suffered?
  was for you and me he paid the cost.

In that lonely grave, there they laid him;
  the disciples were filled with much gloom.
Aren't you glad that old grave could not hold him,
  so on the third day he arose from the tomb?

He went back to his Father in Heaven,
  but he left us a promise behind.
Someday he'd come back for his children.
  Praise God, the hope of sweet Heaven is mine.

A Blanket of Love

Once more the cold wind's blowing
  and the snow is falling down.
Again my thoughts return to Daddy,
  where he sleeps beneath the ground.
The snow will make a blanket
  that will keep my daddy warm.
Wrapped in the arms of Jesus,
  he'll be safe from all the storms.

Each snowflake will remind him
  how he loved this time of year
When we would gather round the fireside,
  he'd tell us all this story there.
How long ago in Bethlehem,
  in a bed made out of hay
A little baby boy was born,
  upon a cold, cold Christmas day.

Remember while you're sleeping, Daddy,
  no greater gift was ever given
Than the one you gave to us
  before you left and went to Heaven.
And as the snow keeps on falling,
  over the place where you now lie
We know you're happy now, dear Daddy,
  you're at home with your Master is why.

The Wonder of Love

I look all around me—at
  the mountains and trees,
See all the flowers,
  the birds and the bees.
I know someone's watching
  from Heaven above
On the world he created,
  and gave with his love.

But we take for granted
  the blessings he gives.
The breath that we're breathing
  each day that we live,
The sun in the morning
  that shines on the dew
Are just some of the things,
  he gave me and you.

The trust in the eyes
  of a sweet baby so dear,
Just a bundle of joy
  he gave us to share.
For what he has done,
  we can never repay.
He gave us his Son
  to show us the way.

He sent him to Calvary
  to die on the cross
So we could have life;
  yes, he paid the cost.
But the greatest gift
  that makes my heart sing—
Our sins were forgiven
  by Jesus, our King.

Marriage Has No Morals Today

Boys and girls of today
  have no morals, it seems.
They don't wait for true love,
  they have their own dreams,
Like living together awhile
  to see how it all works out.
They say a piece of paper
  is not what love's all about.

They think it's old-fashioned
  to take each other for life.
No one tries very hard
  to be a good husband or wife.
Back when I was still young,
  we stayed together like we should,
Took the bad times as well
  as the times that were good.

For God intended it that way
  when man and woman were wed.
To stay together no matter
  how many tears that were shed.
They loved and they cherished
  each other way back then
But now there's so many
  that's living together in sin.

They get married today
  without love in their heart.
If it doesn't always work out,
  then they say they can part.
They don't honor the vows
  that God gave them to say,
That's why so many marriages
  end in divorce today.

Mother's Advice

You're starting on a journey,
  the way won't always be smooth
But if you really love each other,
  there's no way you can lose.
You've already been so blessed
  with a part of his great love.
That little bundle you're now having
  was sent to you from God above.

Always cherish one another
  when temptations come your way.
The vows that you have spoken
  will mean more to you each day.
Say them often to each other and
  your love will keep on growing strong.
Take the bad times with the good
  and you never will go wrong.

If you need to talk to someone,
  just remember I'll be there.
For a child never gets too old
  for Mom to wipe away the tears.
You may think I am old-fashioned,
  but one thing please understand.
I'm proud to be your mother,
  for now I know that you're a man.

Our Years Together

We started on a long sweet journey
  down the bridal path of love.
The day that you and I were married,
  it seemed God blessed us from above.

He gave us faith and understanding
  that helped to make us into one.
We always thought about each other,
  Oh, those first few years were fun.

Then along came our little babies,
  each special in their separate ways.
Oh, we both were so contented
  as we watched them while they played.

At times we thought we couldn't make it
  when things all seemed to turn out wrong
But maybe God was only testing us
  to see if our love was true and strong.

As we walk on down this road of life,
  our children have all grown and gone.
God may have to slow our footsteps,
  but he'll let our love live on.

Where Sweet Roses Will Bloom

Sometimes I get so sad and so weary,
  My heart is so heavy with gloom.
I want to walk through the gardens of Heaven,
  Where forever sweet roses will bloom.

Where there'll be no more heartaches up yonder,
  Never again will my eyes fill with tears.
I'll be happy in the mansion he promised,
  When my loved ones come, new roses appear.

For the roses are a symbol of Heaven.
  It's the flower that God loves so much.
There's miles and miles of little rosebuds
  That God blesses with his tender touch.

I have loved ones who have gone on to Glory.
  They're blooming in the Master's bouquet.
But I'll know them when I walk through the garden;
  They'll be shining in a new kind of way.

Down here they only grow for a season;
  The petals start falling too soon.
But up there in God's beautiful garden,
  Through eternity sweet roses will bloom.

Just a Tiny Rosebud

A little baby boy was
  laid to rest today
To be just a flower for
  the Master's bouquet.
Though you will miss him
  and loved him so much,
Remember he was born
  with God's tender touch.

As a mother you held him
  close with a smile,
But God only loaned him
  to you for a while.
Though you couldn't keep
  him, your bundle of love,
You can meet him again,
  there in Heaven above.

Just a bud of a rose
  in the Master's bouquet.
With the angels in Heaven,
  he's now happy today.
Laughing and singing
  with such pride and joy.
In the arms of sweet Jesus
  sits your darling little boy.

Grandmother's Roses

Oh friends, take a look at my garden.
All the different little roses you see
Each year they just keep on growing,
They always seem ever sweeter to me.

Look at the two tiny rosebuds
That will be in my garden this year.
God must know how much I love roses,
For he just keeps on planting them here.

I pray my garden will go on growing
With baby roses that I love so much.
I'll water them each day with my teardrops,
But God will bless them with his tender touch.

So, children, give Mother my roses.
I know they're God's, but let me enjoy them a while
It's my grandchildren who make up my garden.
It gets more precious each time that one smiles.

Treat my little roses with kindness.
To keep on growing they need all your love,
For the ones you're now giving Mother
Will be beautiful in her bouquet above.

God's Little Rosebuds

I wish that I could see beyond
the sky so clear and blue.
See God up there in his Heaven,
watching over me and you,
Where miles and miles of rosebuds,
far as your eyes can see
Makes you know there is no place
as pretty as Heaven must be.

Each little rosebud is an angel
in God's beautiful bouquet.
I knew they were so happy, for I
watched them while they played.
Not one little child was crippled,
each the same as all the rest
And that's how we all must be
if we expect to be so blessed.

They didn't need any moon or stars,
God's lovelight shone so bright.
The sun was always shining
where there never comes any night
All of the little rosebuds were
the ones we loved so much.
But I know they're happy now for
they've felt the Master's touch.

Fairest of Flowers

A rose is just a flower,
but it's the fairest of all.
It blooms through the summer
and into the early fall.
One sweethearts give each other
to declare their endless love
And it's what God calls his angels
up there in Heaven above.

Its fragrance is like no other
flower that's ever been made
But it's the quickest to wither,
its beauty starts to fade.
We're just like the little rose,
our life here is soon gone.
That's why God calls his roses,
takes them to their new home.

Little babies are rosebuds
in life's beautiful bouquet.
God loans them for a while;
too soon he calls them away.
When the petals start falling,
oh, we know it's much too soon.
So please enjoy all the roses
while their beauty is in bloom.

Darling, when you lay me down
to cross over Canaan's land,
Just take a tiny rosebud
and place it in my hand.
They've been my favorite flower
for all these many long years.
They'll be a symbol of your love,
so please don't shed any tears.

Autumn Time

The leaves are turning brown
  with pretty shades of gold.
The clouds are dark and heavy,
  the weather's turning cold.
But my heart is very happy,
  for Autumn time is here.
To me that's something special,
  it's the best time of the year.

It's time to reap the harvest
  we've worked so hard to grow.
To gather all the pumpkins
  so all the kids will know
Halloween will soon be here
  with ghosts and goblins wild
When I like to watch the face
  of a little wide-eyed child.

It's the time I always like to go
  back to my little country home.
As a child back in the hills,
  I loved so much to roam,
Sit down with the ones I love,
  around the fire at night
Talk about the good times,
  until the morning light.

Time to gather around the table
  on Thanksgiving Day.
Thank God for the many blessings
  he bestowed along the way.
I want to say a special prayer
  and thank him from the start
For giving us the time of year
  I love with all my heart.

A Lonesome Whippoorwill

I awoke to such s sound this morning,
there perched upon my window sill.
Such mournful singing I'd never heard
was from a lonely little whippoorwill.

As I listened, I began to wonder,
had he lost his mate in flight?
Was he just like me, just passing time
to make it through one more lonely night?

It seemed he looked at me as if to say,
like you I've lost my love so dear
How can God up there in his Heaven
leave us both alone down here?

He must have sent that little whippoorwill,
to make me forget troubles of my own.
Although his singing was so lonesome,
it made my little house a home.

So many years have passed since then;
the lonely times are few and brief.
I think about that little whippoorwill,
who helped me make it through my grief.

I wonder has he found himself a new love,
is he singing a happy song today?
To me he deserves the best there is;
I thank God for sending him my way.

A Tree

A tree can be lots of things:
a beauty to behold,
A place to stop and rest a while
underneath the boughs so low
Where sweethearts like to meet
and talk about their endless love
While birds are singing softly,
high in their nests above.

It can be a little shrub,
or a tall lonesome pine
Standing out in an orchard
with fruit trees of all kinds.
A big old maple out in the yard
with a swing out on a limb
Can be a place for lots of fun
for either her or him.

But the prettiest one I know
is the little dogwood tree.
The one the cross was made from,
where Jesus died for me.
Each spring when it's in bloom,
it fills me with such joy,
For the legend of the dogwood tree,
I heard about when just a boy.

Are Squirrels Smarter than Men?

I walked out in the sunlight
  yesterday and this was what I saw.
A little squirrel was playing
  with a nut crammed in his jaw.
It looked like he was laughing,
  oh how funny he did look.
If I could have taken a picture,
  I think I could have written a book.

He knew that I was watching him,
  for he scampered up a tree.
I swear he must have giggled
  as he ran away from me.
He must have thought that he was
  smart. I almost heard him say,
"I'll fix it so she won't know
  where I'll hide my nuts today."

He must have known that old man
  winter was about to come along.
He scampered up and down that
  tree, happily singing his little song.
I wonder why God made animals
  smarter than he ever made man.
They store treasures for winter,
  while man does the best he can.

They store enough food away
  till spring comes once again.
That's more than I can say for man;
  he seems to spend all that he can.
He sits and worries everyday
  and wonders what he's going to do.
But that little squirrel just sits there,
  so eagerly watching me and you.

What a Little Bird Can Tell You

I marveled as I watched a little bird
  try out his brand-new wings today.
Made me think of my dear Savior
  as he found me stumbling along the way.
Somehow that little bird was just like me
  before he learned just how to fly.
But since sweet Jesus came along,
  my spirit soars beyond the sky.

That little bird kept trying so hard;
  he didn't give up until he flew.
That's more than I can say for man;
  they don't put enough in what they do.
If they can't do the things they try,
  they just give up and let it go.
That's not the way that God intended;
  he made the way so we would know.

He sent his Son down here to die
  so we could have a right to choose.
If we'd open up our hearts to him,
  there's now a way that we can lose.
Like that little bird that kept on trying
  that's just what we all should do.
For if God had given up on us,
  where would that leave me and you?

Through Eyes of Beauty

I saw as I glanced out my window
the prettiest sight I'd ever seen.
The trees were all so lovely
in their pretty shades of green.
Little squirrels were all playing
upon the trapeze wires so high.
I knew God must be watching
from Heaven's window in the sky.

All the birds were gathered round,
waiting for their daily bath.
If you stopped awhile to listen,
you could almost hear them laugh.
How could anyone not like to hear
the songs the little robins sing
As they go about their work?
Oh, what joy to me they bring.

The flowers were all blooming;
oh, what fragrance fills the air
As the little hummingbird pauses
and just seems to flutter there.
I marveled at the honeybee
as he went from flower to flower,
Wondering how much honey he could make,
after working for just one hour.

Just looking at all this beauty
brought a teardrop to my eye,
Made me wonder just how long
anyone could go on asking *why*.
If they'd open up their hearts,
let some sunshine through the door,
This world would be more beautiful
than it's ever been before.

God's Book of Life

In God's great book of life,
  for everyone he keeps a page.
From the day that we're born,
  until we become of age
Every time that we did wrong
  our Blessed Savior knew.
He writes down everything
  he's heard us say and do.

All the places that we go,
  the good deeds that we do
He knows and understands
  if our heart to him is true.
If we let our light shine
  for a stranger along the way,
We'll know all about it
  when we reach Heaven someday.

He has marked the day
  when our life on earth is done.
If we keep our faith in him,
  someday we'll see his Son.
Only he knows the minute,
  the exact time when it will be.
I want to hear him say,
  "Well done, come unto me."

When our loved ones die,
  our hearts are filled with grief.
But he crosses off one more page
  with tears of sweet relief.
They're just another flower
  for his beautiful bouquet.
From God's book of life,
  I hope he calls my name someday.

Homesick for Heaven

O Lord, I'm so tired and so weary,
  my body grows more feeble each day.
But I'll keep pressing onward
  to the light at the end of the way.
When I get home to that city,
  my troubles on earth will be over.
No more pain will I suffer,
  up there on Heaven's bright shore.

Sometimes I feel so discouraged,
  it seems that my friends have all gone.
But I know it will be worth it
  when I reach my eternal home.
The ones that have gone on to Glory
  will be waiting to welcome me there
Yes, I'll keep pressing onward,
  till I reach that city foursquare.

My children are straying from Jesus;
  will they ever find his sweet love?
Will they want to meet Mother
  up there in her new home above?
Where once more we'll be together,
  I'll hold them close to my breast
When I see them someday over yonder,
  in the land of the pure and the blessed.

There'll be peace and contentment;
  no more heartaches there will I see,
For Jesus will be there waiting
  in the mansion he promised to me.
The flowers will be blooming forever
  there in the sweet Master's bouquet.
Each time a new one he'll gather
  will shine brighter for him everyday.

I'm Going to That Country

I am going to that country
  where the sun will always shine.
There I'll see the blessed Savior,
  who washed away these sins of mine.
Where the mansion he has promised
  is awaiting me on high.
Yes, I'm going to that country,
  when I bid this world good-bye.

My friends and my loved ones,
  who've gone before me one by one,
I know they'll be waiting
  to welcome me when I get home
They have safely crossed old Jordan.
  Jesus led them by the hand.
Yes, I'm going to that country,
  over in the promised land.

Where a river is flowing
  with milk and honey, I'm told.
The walls are of jasper;
  the streets are made of gold.
There'll be no more heartaches,
  no more burdens to bear.
Yes, I'm going to that country;
  children, will you meet me there?

Until I Reach Heaven

Lord, I'm asking if you'll hear my plea,
  Will you give me the strength to go on?
It seems they've all turned against me,
  Am I worthy to be one of your own?

Let me feel your sweet love here beside me.
  In everything I do and what I may say,
Lead me just one more step up that mountain,
  Where sweet Heaven won't be far away.

My feet may get weary and stumble, but
  You can set them on the way that is straight.
Holding to your hand you will lead me,
  Until I reach yonder Heaven's fair gate.

I may not see the road that I'm walking,
  So light it with your endless love.
Keep the way so bright I can't lose it;
  Let my faith lead me to Heaven above.

When I get there I'll have a new body,
  Trade this old robe for one that is new.
All my pain and heartaches will be over
  When I bid this world of sorrow adieu.

Symbol of a Man

He was a kind and gentle person
who always seemed to understand
The wants and needs of others,
just the symbol of a man.

We never heard him say a cross word,
or speak unkind of any man.
He always smiled and said hello;
offered to lend a helping hand.

He would always come to help us
when we needed something done.
He would hold and rock the babies,
with him they seemed to have such fun.

He was so happy and full of life;
in his little garden he would roam.
His old hound dogs would stay beside him,
watching over that old cabin home.

But now he's somewhere up in Heaven,
singing around the great white throne.
With all his loved ones gone before him,
he's with them now in his new home.

Your Purpose for Me

Lord, I think I know the agony
  you went through there on the cross.
For I've been down in the valley
  and I thought my soul was lost,
But you reached and pulled me out
  so many times. I wonder why?
You must have had a purpose
  for not wanting me to die.

What was that purpose, Lord,
    or would you have me know?
Was it because I prayed so hard,
  or because I love my children so?
I'd like to see them all come in
  before you call me to come home.
But the job will be so hard,
  they won't even heed you calling, "Come."

You'd leave the ninety and nine
  just for one small little sheep.
Can I do any less than you
  for all the ones defying me?
He stays out on the hillside,
  just far enough from the fold.
But I'll always go on praying
  for his dark and troubled soul.

God, show me with your mercy,
  what you think that I should do.
I love that little sheep so much,
  Lord, I'm leaving it all up to you.
With your sweet and tender mercy
  I know you'll bring the lost ones home.
That's your kind of challenge,
  to save just one more little one.

He Knows All about Me

While standing by my window,
  looking upward toward the skies,
I knew God was up there watching
  me with his ever-seeing eyes.
He knew what I was thinking
  deep down inside my heart.
I hope the way I'm now feeling
  from my soul will never part.

The love I felt for him
  in my heart it put a song
But I didn't have to tell him,
  for he knew it all along.
When I kneel down on my knees,
  he knows before I start to pray
Everything I stand in need of,
  not just what I need today.

All the deeds I may be doing
  as I help some troubled soul,
He knows all my intentions,
  that sweet Heaven is my goal.
The words I speak to someone,
  his tender voice will be my guide.
Every step I may be taking,
  he will be there by my side.

If I should meet a stranger
  as I journey on my way.
Give me words of wisdom, Lord,
  let me know just what to say.
He knows I want to help them,
  so my light will always shine.
Maybe to some poor lost sinner,
  it will give him peace of mind.

Jesus Is My Shepherd

I have someone who loves me,
  who always watches over me.
Just another pilgrim,
  one more little sheep,
One who lets me praise him,
  forever keeps my spirits high.
Sweet Jesus is my shepherd
  and I'll see him by and by.

Yes, Jesus is my shepherd.
  oh, I love him, this I know.
He took my robe of sin
  and washed it white as snow.
I put my trust in him
  when from sin he set me free.
Yes, Jesus is my shepherd,
  he's always watching over me.

Each night when I close my eyes,
  he'll keep me safe from harm.
I'll be resting on his bosom,
  wrapped in his loving arms.
Everyday he'll walk beside me,
  his sweet spirit I will feel.
Jesus is my shepherd,
  oh, I'm so glad he's real.

Through the lonesome valley,
  he'll hold onto my hands.
We'll walk the green pastures
  that lead to Glory land
Across old chilly Jordan,
  the river deep and wide.
Yes, Jesus is my shepherd;
  he'll stay close by my side.

The Deeds He Had Done

Did the Lord ever get so discouraged
  When he walked this old earth as a man?
Did he ever cry or beg for God's mercy
  Or did he just say, "I understand."

As he so humbly walked among sinners,
  Did he ever turn his back upon one?
They mocked and they scorned him while teaching,
  But so faithfully, he kept pressing on.

He healed the sick and the crippled,
  The eyes of the blind, he made them see.
But yet so many didn't believe him,
  They wondered, "What kind of man could he be?"

He walked hundreds of miles on his travels.
  Oh, how weary he must have become.
He blessed everyone who would curse him.
  So meekly he bore all the shame.

He loved the little children so dearly,
  He held each one close to his heart.
That's why he wants us to raise them the right way,
  When they grow old, from it they'll never depart.

But soon it came time and he knew it.
  One more job that would be the last one.
When he carried our burdens up to Calvary,
  He knew the will of his Father had been done.

I Traded It All for Jesus

For so long I was wandering in darkness,
  Old Satan had a good hold on me.
I loved all the pleasures he offered,
  I was wretched and vile as could be.

Then one day I heard someone whisper,
  "Oh, my child, will you let me come in?
Take a good look at where you are going,
  if you don't let me save you from sin."

I'd never before heard a voice like it;
  the words he said to me were so sweet
I bowed down and begged for his mercy,
  and I found it at my Savior's feet.

I gave my heart and soul to Jesus
  who gave his life upon that old tree.
His blood that he shed was for sinners.
  Lord I'm so glad that included me.

I gave up this world full of heartaches,
  all the pleasures old Satan could hold.
I've just traded them all for a mansion
  up there in that city of gold.

He Saved a Sinner like Me

I was just a lonely sinner
who'd been wandering for so long
Out in this world of darkness
with no friends to call my own.
No place to rest my weary soul
as I went from door to door,
But the Lord had plans for me,
now I'm so happy ever more.

Unlike all the many others,
I thought I was just too small.
For I felt I was unworthy,
the least one among them all.
But he showed me with his sweet love
just how much my soul was worth.
Now I'm feeling oh, so happy,
I'm the proudest one on earth.

I now have a loving Savior
who walks and talks with me.
As I travel on my journey,
I have never felt so free.
He takes my hand and leads me
when I stumble along the way.
I know he'll keep me in his care
till I reach my home someday.

I will sing there with the angels
around the great white throne
With all my friends and loved ones
who have gone before me one by one.
My precious old Mother and Daddy,
they will know me, this I know.
I will have a smile awaiting
just for them at Heaven's door.

Don't They Want Jesus?

They crucified our Savior,
they nailed him to the cross.
He gave up his own life
for a world that was lost.
His arms are wide open,
pleading for every man
To give up his sins and
join him in Heaven's land.

He hung there on the tree,
his eyes cast on Heaven's shore.
The blood that he shed
was for sins that we bore.
Men turn their backs on him,
when they hear his gentle call.
Don't they want to go to Heaven
it's the sweetest place of all.

Don't they want his arms around them
when they face the hands of death?
Know he's there beside them
as they draw their final breath?
What will their soul be worth
if they lose it in the end?
Where will they spend eternity
if they're still lost in their sins?

Come and go with me, brother,
where the healing waters flow.
Give up this world of trouble;
trade it for a crown of gold.
The mansion that's awaiting,
there's room for everyone
If we want to go to Heaven,
when our race on earth is run.

Be True to Jesus

The foundation to build on
 is the name of the Lord
We'll have a new life.
 if we believe in his word.
If we stand true to him,
 we won't stumble and fall.
For if we miss Heaven,
 friends, we'll miss it all.

There's nothing to do
 but give up our sins.
Just throw open the door
 and let sweet Jesus come in.
He'll live in our hearts
 and fill it with love
And take us to live
 there in that city above.

We won't be afraid to
 cross the river so wide.
He'll always be with us,
 he'll stay by our side.
Through the valley of death,
 he'll hold to our hand.
Oh, there's nothing to fear,
 if for Jesus we stand.

Let's stand up for Jesus,
 who's steady and strong.
He'll take us to Heaven,
 where we'll sing a new song
There with the archangels
 around the white throne,
We'll live with our loved ones
 up there in our new home.

Because He Cared

I was lost, my world
  was nothing but darkness.
Kept sinking deeper
  everyday in despair.
Then I found someone who
  would always stand beside me.
It was my Savior who
  showed me how much he cared.

My Savior cared enough for me,
  he died at Calvary
Made me an heir to
  a mansion over there.
I can't thank him enough
  for my Salvation.
Now I'm singing every day
  because he cared.

Every night I close my
  eyes, I always wonder,
Will I live to see the
  light of one more day?
If it's his will, that it's
  now time for me to join him,
I'll say, "Lord, because you
  cared, just lead the way."

As I walk that lonesome valley,
  he'll be with me.
My final breath will be
  to whisper one last prayer.
I'll thank him for the blood
  he shed for me at Calvary
To give me everlasting
  life because he cared.

Never a Sweeter Vision

I've never had such a beautiful vision of Heaven.
  There were no street lights to be seen over there,
Just a halo of light shining from Jesus
  That lit up that whole city so fair.

Little children seemed so happy while playing,
  Skipping through the pastures so green,
Their faces were all lit up with such laughter,
  Was the prettiest sight I'd ever seen.

All my loved ones were sitting by the river,
  While singing, their voices blended so sweet.
There were no strangers, they all loved each other.
  With outstretched arms, each new one they'd greet.

I saw Mother and Daddy who'd gone on before me.
  It seemed they'd never parted at all.
They said they'd been waiting so long to see me,
  Prayed many times I wouldn't stumble and fall.

They now owned a mansion in that beautiful city
  With pretty roses entwined round their door.
I could see them both standing, waiting there for me
  To be with them on Heaven's bright shore.

I Heard a Voice Whisper

I was just another sinner,
  I'd reached my journey's end.
I let old Satan lead me on
  down the road of sin.
I laughed at Salvation,
  I lived a life of shame.
But I heard a voice whisper,
  and it softly called my name.

When I heard a voice whisper,
  so softly in my heart,
I knew old-time Salvation
  and me would never part.
I found just what I needed
  to make my life complete.
When I heard a voice whisper
  I knew God had spoken to me.

Now I love the things I hated,
  and I hate the things I loved.
That sweet old-time religion,
  Lord I just can't get enough.
Each night I close my eyes
  and pray that I will be
Worthy of that whisper
  that he bestowed on me.

Now my Lord is walking with me
  as I journey on my way.
I've got a mansion waiting
  and I'll reach it some sweet day.
I'll praise his name forever,
  thank him when I get home
For that soft and gentle whisper
  that's always kept me pressing on.

Am I Worthy of His Love?

O sinners, let me tell you
  what Salvation means to me.
I've become a new creature,
  from sin I've been set free.
My loving Savior holds me
  in the palm of his hand,
Tells me that he loves me,
  this unworthy little man.

Yes, I'm unworthy, so unworthy
  to be called my Savior's son.
The least one of his creaturs
  underneath the shining sun.
But I know that he loves me,
  for the Bible tells me so
And that makes me worthy,
  of my Savior's love, I know.

I've been washed in the blood
  of God's precious holy Son
Who died upon the rugged tree,
  gave his life to give me one.
Now I'm singing praises to him
  everyday while here I live.
Someday I'll go and see him,
  there's more blessings he will give.

There I'll see my loved ones,
  who have gone on before.
My blessed old mother and daddy
  will be waiting at the door.
I'm sure that they will know me
  by the smile that I'll wear.
When I get home to that mansion,
  they'll meet me over there.

All Because

Lord, to me there's never
been a dearer friend
Since you reached down
and saved me from a life of sin.
On that old cross you
bore such pain and agony,
All because you loved
someone like me.

You gave up your home
in glory I know.
Came to earth to walk
among men here below.
Though they mocked you and
scorned your precious name,
All because of them
you bore all the shame.

They drove nails through
your precious hands.
Yet you loved them though
they couldn't understand.
The blood flowed freely
as they pierced your side.
"Forgive them, Father," were
the words they heard you cry.

Get down on your knees
and seek this friend of mine.
Give him your heart
while yet there is still time.
The hope of Heaven
can be yours eternally
All because he shed
his blood at Calvary.

A Crown of Old Thorns

Oh, think of the pain our
  blessed Lord went through
As he hung on the cross
  to give life to me and you.
All the shame that he bore as
  they mocked him and scorned
When they placed on his head
  a crown of old thorns.

Just a crown of old thorns
  he wore round his head.
But yet it was for us,
  when, "Forgive them," he said.
How can you refuse him
  after all he has borne
As the blood came from
  a crown of old thorns.

They nailed his dear hands
  to that old rugged cross.
God gave his only Son
  so we would not be lost.
Wasn't it enough? All
  the blood that he shed
Without placing a crown
  of old thorns on his head?

What our Lord went through
  we can never repay.
But give up your sins,
  you can see him someday.
When you get to Heaven,
  on your head he'll adorn
A crown of pure gold,
  not a crown of old thorns.

What If?

I arose from my bed just this morning
  and bowed there on my bended knees.
What if my God in his Heaven
  hadn't saved a wretched sinner like me?

What if on the cross where they nailed him,
  they hadn't driven nails in his hands?
What if the blood he shed there on Calvary
  was all in vain; what should we do then?

What if in our times of trials and troubles
  we had no one else to turn to?
When we get down so low in the valley,
  what if he's not there to see us through?

What if our hearts couldn't find him,
  he didn't hear when we knelt down to pray.
What if he just said it wasn't worth it;
  oh, tell me what should we do today?

What if when cold death came to claim us,
  he wasn't there to be close by our side?
What if our hands he won't be holding,
  when we cross Jordan's river so wide?

What if our eyes can never see Heaven,
  when it's time to say our last prayer?
What if he should turn his back upon us;
  what will we do if we can't find Jesus there?

Mary's Son's Birthday

Well, here it is again, Dear Jesus,
  your birthday's come and passed.
How many thought about you,
  or was today just like the last
When as a little baby you were born
  upon this day so many years ago
There in a little manger,
  in Bethlehem, we all know.

I wonder if your mother knew
  the day that you were born.
Did she think about the heartaches
  that bright and early morn?
With Joseph and the wise men,
  all the animals gathered round,
Was her mind so occupied,
  she hid the tears falling down.

Did she know that you were born
  to one day become a king?
Did she think of running away,
  hiding with you above everything?
She must have known, or else her
  will was stronger than our own.
Could we give up one of ours,
  let him die upon the cross alone?

But thank you for your birthday, Jesus,
  for now it means so much to me.
I know you did a lot of suffering
  there to set this sinner free.
And, Mary, if you're listening,
  you know where my thoughts lie.
Give your Son a kiss for me
  and I'll see you when I die.

Gift of Mary's Love

Jesus Christ was born there
  in a manger many years ago,
While stars twinkled brightly
  outside upon the snow.
Mary wrapped him in a blanket
  and laid him there upon the hay
That made up that little cradle
  where sweet baby Jesus lay.

Wise men came from near and far
  just to look upon his face.
They were guided by a star
  that led them to the place.
How proud Mary must have been
  as she held him in her arms.
All the animals gathered round
  to keep that baby safe and warm.

He walked here upon this earth
  for thirty some odd years.
I know that Mother Mary
  must have shed so many tears.
She knew her Son would have to die
  to save a world from being lost.
Oh, how she must have suffered
  as she looked upon the cross.

When she watched her darling Son
  take that walk up Calvary Hill,
Can you put yourself in her place,
  just imagine how she must feel?
Don't you think she must have wanted
  to take him and hold him close?
Take his place upon the cross,
  all because she loved him so?

But I'm so glad that he was born
  to die upon that old rugged cross.
Without him there'd be no Heaven;
  our souls forever would be lost.
At the expense of a mother's pain,
  we have the hope of a home above.
I thank God with all my heart
  for the gift of Mary's sweet love.

Waiting for Christmas

It's that time of year again,
  everyone is full of cheer.
For just around the corner,
  Christmas will soon be here.
The snowflakes will be falling
  so softly to the ground.
Sleigh bells will be ringing
  in my little old home town.

The trees will be decorated,
  so pretty, bright, and gay.
Little children everywhere
  are just waiting for that day.
They seem to know pretty soon
  old Santa Claus will be there,
Bringing lots and lots of toys
  in answer to their prayers.

Mama will be in the kitchen
  baking delicious pumpkin pies,
Daddy gently watching her
  with a twinkle in his eyes.
A stocking's hung beside the fire
  for each and every child.
There's not so long to wait,
  now it's only a little while.

The children will be nodding
  their little sleepy heads.
Covered up so snugly
  each in their own little beds
Waiting for Christmas morning
  when they all can finally see
What old Santa Claus has left
  underneath their little tree.

Well, Christmas day is finally here,
  and just look at what I see.
Lots of happy, smiling faces
  all around the Christmas tree,
Jumping up and down for joy,
  for their wish has just come true.
If everyday could be like Christmas,
  we'd like to have it all year through.

Love Thy Neighbor

Don't be too quick to judge that
  man who's drinking all alone.
He might have lost everything
  that once he called his own.
Take those thoughts that you may
  have and put them on the shelf.
But for the mercy of your God,
  he could have been yourself.

A lot of loving memories now
  may be messing up his mind.
That bottle he's now holding
  is the only comfort he can find.
That big old house is now empty
  that he used to call his home.
The patter of little feet,
  he now misses since they're gone.

He hates to even go back home,
  the pain's too great to bear.
No smiles to greet him at the door,
  no kisses waiting there.
Just put yourself in his place,
  think how lonely he must be
With nothing but the bottle
  to help forget his memories.

He just needs to have someone
  to gently hold his hand.
One word of understanding
  to make him feel like he's a man.
Let him know he's not alone,
  you're there to be his friend.
For what would God think of you
  if you turned your back on him!

Keep Our Boys from Harm

O Lord, watch over our boys
who are fighting with sorrow and care.
Reach down your arms and protect them
and bring them to us back here.

For like Mary once held baby Jesus
so tightly in her loving arms,
Just like her, we've held our babies,
So would you please keep them from harm?

They're fighting to save this old country,
but sometimes the hope seems so dim.
Will they put their trust in sweet Jesus
and start to honor old Glory again?

It's so hard when we see them marching,
off to a war that's made only by man
That's why mothers will keep praying
there'll be nothing but love through this land.

No more blood would have to be shed;
no more battles would have to be won.
There'd be peace all over this country
if they knew the love of God's Son.

Just a Nurse's Aide

It seems that as a nurse's aide,
  we're not thought of very much.
But as for me I wouldn't trade it,
  my reward is just a gentle touch.

By reaching out and helping someone
  who seems so sad and all alone,
It always makes me very happy
  to know I have my job well done.

Girls, before you brush that hand away
  that's reaching out for understanding,
Just remember those hands were once
  so very gentle and undemanding.

Those hands and arms once held a baby
  with all the love and trust they had.
So before you speak and say a cross word,
  stop and think, *This could be Mom or Dad.*

Drinking's the Devil

In this wicked old world,
  it gets harder each day.
Old Satan keeps trying
  to take over some way.
Well, drinking's the devil
  that's ruined my home
And old Satan is laughing,
  another soul he has won.

For everytime that I pray,
  he's laughing at me.
He says lots of things,
  while I'm on my knees.
If drinking's the devil,
  then I'm living with one.
But Glory to God,
  I'm still singing his song.

That little girl of mine
  asked me a question one day.
It was so hard to swallow,
  when I heard her say,
"Mommy, tell me, does God
  ever answer any prayers?
I've been praying for Daddy,
  but I guess he doesn't hear."

I said, "Just keep praying.
  God hears every prayer
Just keep trusting in him;
  he's always right there.
It may take some time,
  but one day Daddy will see
That drinking's the devil,
  and it always will be."

Getting Too Old

Lord, my heart is full of sorrow
  as I look along the way.
Many things keep troubling me
  as I journey day by day.
My children are all straying,
  how do I bring them to the fold?
Do I just keep on praying?
  You've got to help, I'm growing old.

I'm growing old and this old body
  isn't what it used to be.
But let me stay a little longer,
  a little strength just give to me.
Oh, I know I cannot make it
  without your blessed hand to hold,
So I'm trusting in you, Jesus,
  help me while I'm growing old.

Show them as they stray here,
  in this big old world of sin,
They'll have nothing but playthings
  to look back where they've been.
Let them see the light ahead
  and just let that be their guide,
Then I know they will make it,
  as long as you are by their side.

Though my steps may stumble, Jesus,
  and my eyes get almost blind,
Please let them all follow you
  if I should leave them behind.
Let them see the gates of Heaven,
  walk the straight and narrow road.
Then I can go to sleep in peace,
  for Mother's getting much too old.

Waiting for a Brighter Day

There's a brighter day a-coming,
  Lord, don't let it be too long.
Let the sun shine a little brighter,
  let me sing just one more song,
Let me live a little longer,
  by maybe just a few more days.
All my children are still out there;
  too many things are in their way.

They are waiting at the wayside,
  knowing not which way to turn
Show them, Lord, with your sweet mercy
  the only way that leads to home.
Let them see that all their pleasures
  are just playthings here below.
For without you I am nothing;
  I'm trying my best to let them know.

Let them look at that old crossroad
  like Mom and Daddy had to do.
It's so hard to choose the right one,
  but your help will pull them through.
From the one that leads to destruction,
  turn their feet the other way
Toward the one that leads to Heaven,
  Where Mother's waiting by the gate.

There's a Better Day Coming

There's a better day a-coming;
  Lord, I feel it in my soul.
Christ will come and gather roses
  as he takes his daily stroll.
So, Mother, please be patient,
  the time won't be too long.
There's a better day a-coming,
  when he'll take his children home.

I often think about my daddy;
  never once heard him complain.
As he lay and suffered down here,
  how he must have felt the pain,
But he kept his eyes toward Heaven,
  for he knew what lay in store
Was a better day a-coming;
  he wouldn't suffer any more.

How can we be any different
  if our God's the same as his?
Though afflictions come upon us,
  we can pray the way he did.
Be a true and faithful servant,
  another rose for his bouquet.
There's a better day a-coming
  and we'll make it there someday.

He will put no more upon us
  than he knows that we can bear.
I just steal away somewhere
  and I kneel to him in prayer.
Let me be more understanding
  if this old pain won't go away.
There's a better day a-coming,
  where sweet roses never fade.